The Shortcut to Scholastic Latin

Copyright © 2019 Dylan Schrader

All rights reserved. No part of this book may be reproduced, stored, or transmitted by any means—whether auditory, graphic, mechanical, or electronic—without written permission of both publisher and author, except in the case of brief excerpts used in critical articles and reviews. Unauthorized reproduction of any part of this work is illegal and is punishable by law.

Copyright © 2019 Paideia Institute for Humanistic Study, Inc.

All rights reserved.

First Edition, First Printing: 2019

ISBN: 978-1734018929

The Paideia Institute for Humanistic Study, Inc.
www.paideiainstitute.org

TABLE OF CONTENTS

CHAPTER I
Quidditas: About This Guide 1
   What Is the Purpose of This Guide? 2
   How Does This Guide Work? 2
   What Will This Guide Not Do? 2

CHAPTER II
Tolle, Lege: What Am I Reading? 4
   The Speaking behind the Writing 4
   The Writing behind the Printing 5
   The Reading behind the Writing 6

CHAPTER III
Distinguendum Est: Breaking Things Up 8
   Back and Forth 11

CHAPTER IV
Sic Proceditur: The Passive and Impersonal Passive 13
   The Simple Passive 13
   The Impersonal Passive 13

CHAPTER V
Obiter Dicta: Indirect Discourse and Substantive Clauses 15
   Indirect Discourse 15
   Substantive Clauses 15

CHAPTER VI
Res Sic Se Habet: Some Peculiarities 19
   Not So Strict about the Subjunctive 19
   Comparative Adjectives in the Ablative End in -i 20
   The Gerund Often Takes the Place of the Gerundive 20
   The Comparative Often Serves as the Superlative 22
   Perfect Passive Participles in the Conjugation
   of Verbs Are Treated Like Adjectives 22

CHAPTER VII
Locutiones: **Key Expressions** 23

CHAPTER VIII
Non Habet Locum:
Foreign Influences, Calques, and Technical Terms 33

CHAPTER IX
Caeteris Deficientibus: **When All Else Fails** 36
    Strategy 1: Search within the Text 36
    Strategy 2: Google Book Search or Google Web Search 36
    Strategy 3: Topical Web Search 36
    Strategy 4: Use the Resource List 37
    Strategy 5: Phone a Friend 37
    Strategy 6: Stay the Course 37

CHAPTER X
Sample Text 1 38

CHAPTER XI
Sample Text 2 53

CHAPTER XII
Sample Text 3 59

CHAPTER XIII
Resource List 63

CHAPTER I
Quidditas: About This Guide

There are thousands of manuscripts and printed volumes of Scholastic works for a reason. It is because countless authors found themselves in the situation that we ourselves do whenever we tackle truly important questions. As Peter Abelard (1079–1142) observed:

> | Sed dum quaerimus quaestiones expedire difficiliores fortassis incurrimus controversias; et dum quosdam dissolvimus nodos, aliis fortioribus nos alligamus.[1] | But when we seek to resolve questions, perhaps we run into more difficult controversies. And when we untangle certain knots, we end up tying ourselves up in even stronger ones. |
> | --- | --- |

The majority of the Scholastic works that address these important questions exist only in Latin. This guide is written for students, seminarians, researchers, teachers, and others who want to engage with Scholastic texts in Latin, particularly those concerned with philosophy and theology. It presumes you have intermediate knowledge of Latin and of the topics being discussed in the Scholastic texts you want to read. If you have studied Latin but find Scholastic idiom and style difficult, this guide is for you.

Here's a quick test:

> Propter se dicitur dupliciter. Uno modo secundum quod opponitur ad propter aliud; et hoc modo virtutes et honestum non propter se diliguntur, cum etiam ad aliud referantur. Alio modo dicitur propter se, secundum quod opponitur ad per accidens; et sic dicitur propter se diligi quod habet in natura sua aliquid movens ad diligendum: et hoc modo virtutes propter se diliguntur, quia habent in se aliquid unde quaerantur, etsi nihil aliud ab eis contingeret: non tamen est inconveniens ut aliquid propter se ametur et tamen ad alterum ordinetur, sicut dicitur in 1 *Ethic.* Est autem aliquid quod desideratur, non propter aliquid quod in se habet, sed tantum secundum quod ordinatur ad alterum, ut effectivum illius; sicut potio amara amatur, non propter aliquid quod in ipsa est, sed quia sanitatem efficit: et

---

1 Peter Abelard, *Theologia summi boni.*

> huiusmodi nullo modo propter se diliguntur; sive propter se dicat causam formalem, sicut virtus dicitur propter se diligi; sive finalem, sicut Deus.[2]

If you know most of the words in this passage and more or less recognize their grammatical features but find it awkward or can't read it smoothly, this guide is for you.

What Is the Purpose of This Guide?

This guide is meant to help someone who has studied Latin grammar read Scholastic texts without great difficulty (at least without great difficulty due to Latin). A secondary goal is to sharpen English translation skills.

How Does This Guide Work?

This guide leads the reader through features of Scholastic Latin with examples from real texts by a variety of authors and on a variety of subjects. Naturally, authors differ somewhat based on their time period, region, and personal style. Further, the texts of a single author will vary based on genre and based on how they have come down to us in the manuscript tradition. Nevertheless, the Scholastics were all able to understand one another's Latin. This was itself one of the pillars of the culture allowing for the development of the schools and inter-school discussions over the course of centuries. Therefore, this guide focuses on the most common structures, quirks, and turns of phrase.

By design, this guide is as succinct and direct as possible. It is only a shortcut to dealing with the general features and peculiarities of Scholastic Latin. This guide is not a formal grammar, nor is it a replacement for what is truly needed to master Scholastic Latin: many hours hearing, speaking, reading, and writing it.

What Will This Guide Not Do?

This guide will *not* teach you the subject matter being discussed in the Scholastic authors you're reading. Nor will it define the various technical terms pertaining to philosophy, theology, or the natural sciences that you will encounter throughout Scholastic texts. The resource list at the end of this guide will point you to further resources that can help in these areas. This guide is only meant to help remove syntactical and stylistic obstacles to Scholastic Latin. By the way, if you're looking to familiarize yourself with

---

2 Thomas Aquinas, *Super I Sent.*, d. 1, q. 2, a. 1, ad 3.

the Scholastic milieu, an entertaining and effective way to start is by reading Umberto Eco's novel, *The Name of the Rose.*

CHAPTER II
Tolle, Lege: What Am I Reading?

The term 'Scholastic Latin' is both narrow and broad. On the one hand, it refers to the Latin that expresses a specific academic method and style not hard to distinguish from other flavors of Latin. On the other hand, it covers countless works of countless authors over a period of about six hundred years (roughly 1200–1800), with a lasting influence on the neo-Scholastic and manualistic Latin of the nineteenth and twentieth centuries. The Scholastics would probably say that *Latinitas Scholastica* is narrow in intension and broad in extension, or that it is unique formally but multiplied materially.

In this chapter, we will make three general observations about the material we are reading when we read Scholastic Latin. First, the written text has its origin in live speech. Second, the printed text has its origin in handwritten texts. Third, the Scholastics' own work draws heavily on previous material.

The Speaking behind the Writing

The first thing that we modern readers must keep in mind is that *all* Scholastic texts have their origin in some way in spoken Latin. In some cases, this means quite directly that what we have as a text really consists of lecture notes (a *lectura*) written by a teacher (*magister*) for his classroom. Or, we might have notes that a student transcribed from the teacher's lesson (a *reportatio*). That transcription might be official, done by a scribe appointed for the task, or it might be unofficial. The teacher might have checked the transcription later on (a *reportatio examinata*) or even re-worked his notes and those of others more fully (an *ordinatio*).

Sometimes, the oral source of the text in front of us comes through plainly:

Diversitas materiae potest accipi dupliciter. **Vel diversitas** partium speciei, idest partium specie differentium, sive formaliter, ut manus, pes, et hujusmodi; et talis diversitas causatur ex parte formae: quia ex hoc quod forma est talis, oportet quod corpus sit sibi sic dispositum.	Differentiation of matter can be taken in two ways. **Either the differentiation** is that of the parts of a species, i.e., of parts differing specifically (formally), such as a hand, a foot, and things of this sort. And this kind of differentiation is caused on the side of the form because from the fact that the form is such-and-such, the body must be disposed for it in a certain way.

Est autem quaedam diversitas materialis tantum, quae ad speciem non pertinet, sed ad individuum tantum; et ista redundat ex materia in formam, et non e converso.³	**But there is also a differentiation** that is only material, which pertains not to the species but to the individual alone. And this latter kind redounds to the form from the matter, not vice versa.

In this example, Thomas Aquinas (1225–74) is distinguishing two ways that one portion of matter can be different from another. One way is that a certain species (like human beings) can require different kinds of material parts (like hands and feet). Another way is that each individual of the same species, while having the same kind of form (humanity), is also constituted by a distinct parcel of matter. In the first way, Peter's human form causes his hand to be different from his foot. In the second way, the fact that Peter is made up of different matter from John causes Peter's and John's human forms to be individually distinct from each other.

What's interesting for our present purposes is that Aquinas began to describe these two possibilities by saying *vel ... vel ...* ('either ... or ... '), but he lost track of what construction he used at the beginning and never uttered the second *vel*. Instead, he finished out his point in a different way: *Est autem quaedam diversitas ...* . This is the kind of minor mistake that all of us make when speaking, and it evidences the fact that Aquinas's commentary here was originally a classroom lecture.

Even works that were written from the start (like Aquinas's *Summa theologiae*) come from the experience of living, teaching, and conversing in the Latin language in a university environment. That milieu is always in the background of the texts. Further, these written works were also destined to prompt subsequent live discussions.

The Writing behind the Printing

Another point to remember is that before the printing press, manuscripts had to be written out and copied by hand. They were literally *manu scripta*. The text we have in front of us may not be exactly what the original author intended. It may contain additions, suffer from omissions, have lost sections, and be permeated with small variations introduced over subsequent centuries by copyists and editors trying to correct one another's mistakes or perpetuating them.

A good modern critical edition will explain in its introduction which manuscript it has used as a base text and how comparisons to other

---

3   Thomas Aquinas, *Super II Sent.*, d. 32, q. 2, a. 3, ad 6.

manuscripts were made and conflicts among them decided. It is often worth looking at the critical apparatus to see what variations exist in the text as we have it.

The Reading behind the Writing

Finally, we should remember that the Scholastic authors had a different view of scholarship and academic dialogue than we do. One of their chief concerns was to reconcile what they took to be authoritative statements by preceding authors. This is an expression of the Scholastic conviction that the truth fits with the truth, which is also why an idea's *convenientia*, its 'fittingness' or 'appropriateness,' counts as evidence for it, whereas elements of *inconvenientia* argue against it. The authorities looked to by the Scholastics were especially the Bible, Church councils, the Church Fathers, liturgical texts, the works of philosophers (especially Aristotle), and experts in other fields (e.g., Galen and Ptolemy). Though Scholastics often allude to or cite these authorities, they usually do so without the detailed information that modern scholarship demands. This can make it hard to find the quotation or supporting statement in question.

Further, we should not assume that all such citations are accurate. Sometimes, a particular Scholastic author had access to copies of the works they were citing, and sometimes they did not. They might have had a collection of important passages or commonplaces or worked from a previously digested commentary, such as a biblical Gloss. They might also cite an authoritative passage based only on its presence in other Scholastic works or copy the list of references given by another Scholastic author without checking them. Even if a Scholastic author had the cited work in front of him, his edition might have been corrupted or spurious.

For example, on the question of whether the union of two natures in Christ is the greatest of all unions, Aquinas cites a passage that he thinks is from Augustine but ends up rejecting it—a rare move for any of the Scholastics.[4] It turns out, however, that the passage in question is spurious and was most likely not from Augustine at all. Here we witness that the deep-seated Scholastic desire to reconcile authorities always takes second place to a longing for the truth.

Actually, we should not lump all the Scholastics together. Most were quite reverential, but some of them had their doubts about whether the authorities

---

4   Compare Thomas Aquinas, *Summa theologiae* III, q. 2, a. 9, sc. to the response that Aquinas gives to the *Sed contra* at the end of the same article. The passage cited is a likely inauthentic variant in some copies of Augustine's *De Trinitate* I.

they believed in so strongly were always reconcilable or even self-consistent. For example, at one point Walter Chatton (ca. 1290–1343) says:

Studere quindecim annis ad concordandum dicta Aristotelis non videtur mihi quod expediat, quia forte adhuc in decimo sexto deficiet quis, licet bene in principio expediat exercitari in dictis eius. Dico quod si argumentum suum valeat, est illud quod feci. Et si sit aliud, glossent eum qui volunt.[5]	Spending fifteen years in academic work to harmonize what Aristotle says doesn't seem to be a good use of time to me, since maybe one would end up failing at it in the sixteenth year, although it is a good use of time to train oneself in his statements at the beginning. I say that if his argument is valid, then it's what I have done. And if it's something else, then let those who wish to gloss him do so.

Now when it comes to their contemporaries, the Scholastics usually behave differently than they do with their authorities. Rather than refer to their colleagues by name, they frequently employ a vague anonymous expression like *quidam dicunt …* ('some say … '). What is worse to the modern reader, the Scholastics often appropriate others' arguments or examples without any indication that these are borrowed. This habit can be annoying to those of us who would like to compare the opposing viewpoints with greater ease.

Again, we must imagine ourselves to be immersed in the living discussion that the written page reflects. Contemporary Scholastics debated one another, talked with one another, taught each other's students, etc. If they said *quidam dicunt*, chances were that everyone involved knew who was being referenced. A modern critical edition can help by filling in some of the missing information.

---

5 Walter Chatton, *Reportatio super I Sent.*, d. 2, q. 4, ad 1.

CHAPTER III
Distinguendum Est: Breaking Things Up

The Scholastic method proceeds by clarifying a precise inquiry, distinguishing it from related points of inquiry, and by examining the arguments from authority and reason for different answers to that inquiry. Often the solution lies in a distinction, especially for an author who is keen to show the harmony among apparently contradictory authorities. In other words, the Scholastic method thrives on precision, and this precision is achieved by back-and-forth discussion.

For example, when addressing the question of whether more than one priest can consecrate the same host, the Salmanticenses (seventeenth-century Discalced Carmelites of Salamanca) begin as follows:

Multis modis intelligi potest, quod plures sacerdotes concurrant ad unius hostiae consecrationem.[6]	There are many ways in which we can understand more than one priest's coming together for the consecration of a single host.

They go on to explain that one priest might intend to consecrate half a host and another the other half or that one priest might intend to consecrate one host only on the condition that another priest intends to consecrate another, etc. In their opinion, all of these situations would require distinct answers.

It is no surprise, then, to find that Scholastic authors are careful to divide their work not only on the macro level (into tractates, disputations, questions, articles, etc.) but also on the micro level. They achieve this latter effect by using otherwise redundant or unnecessary words to emphasize natural breaks within a sentence and by structuring their paragraphs and sections to indicate the back-and-forth of their discussion.

Take the following example (formatted to illustrate the structure):

Sed,	But,
quia scientia omnis principaliter pensanda est ex fine,	because every science is principally to be considered on the basis of the end,

---

6 Salmanticenses, *Cursus theologicus,* tract. 23, disp. 12, dub. 2.

finis **autem** ultimus istius doctrinae est contemplatio primae veritatis in patria,	and the last end of this teaching is the contemplation of the first truth in our heavenly homeland,
ideo principaliter speculativa est.[7]	it is principally speculative.

Here we see how Aquinas not only uses a nice *autem*, which shows that the clause running from *finis … in patria* is a subordinate clause, he also uses *ideo*, which is not necessary grammatically, so that we have *quia A … ideo B*, which in English is just 'because A, B.' Our modern editions give us niceties like commas and other punctuation, but we should put ourselves in the situation of a student reading a hand-copied manuscript or—even better—listening to Aquinas as he lectures on the first book of Peter Lombard's *Sentences*. Hearing *quia*, with an explanatory dip down to the clause marked by *autem*, and then reaching *ideo*, which indicates the follow-up to *quia*, keeps the structure of the whole argument in our mind as the teacher speaks.

Let's take another example, where *tum* is used at the head of sentences to mark out a list of supporting rationales, in this case reasons why the Salmanticenses reject a certain view of how grace is necessary for a person to make an act of faith:

Nec valet praedictus modus consistere in facilitate, ut vult Durandus: **tum quia** Concilia damnant eos, qui asserunt gratiam esse necessariam, ut ea, quae simpliciter per naturam, facilius possimus per gratiam, ut constat ex Milevitano *capite quinto*; sed in sententia, quam impugnamus, gratia solum requiritur ut actus fiat eo modo, quo oportet: ergo hic modus nequit in facilitate consistere. **Tum etiam quia** potentia facile potest elicere actus ad quos habet virtutem completam,	Nor can the aforementioned manner consist in ease, as is Durandus's opinion. **This is because** the councils condemn those who assert that grace is necessary that we may be able to do more easily through grace what we can do through nature simply, as is clear from Milevitanus, chapter 5. But in the opinion that we are impugning, grace is only required that the act be done in the manner necessary. Therefore this manner cannot consist in ease. **This is also because** a potency can easily elicit acts for which it has complete power,

---

7   Thomas Aquinas, *Super I Sent.*, q. 1, a. 3, qc. 1, co.

ut observavimus *Tractatu* 12, *disputat. dubio* 3, *numero* 39, et satis apparet in omnibus actibus eo quod sunt proportionati facultati potentiae: ergo si actus fidei Theologicae secundum suam speciem acceptus est pure naturalis, et perinde proportionatus intellectui nostro, poterit elici faciliter, quin habitus requiratur. **Tum praeterea: quia** facilitas est ejusdem ordinis cum actu, et potest per ipsum repetitum acquiri: ergo si possumus per vires naturales elicere assensum fidei, poterimus etiam per easdem vires comparare facilitatem illius: sed non valemus elicere sicut oportet: ergo ly *sicut oportet* non determinat aliquem modum facilitatis. **Tum denique, quia** ut actus conducat ad salutem, non petit fieri cum facilitate: cujus signum est, quod etsi ex gratia fiat, solet cum difficultate fieri: ergo quod sit, sicut oportet, nequit in modo facilitatis consistere.[8]	as we observed in Tracate 12, disputation 1, doubt 3, number 39, and as is clear enough in all acts by the fact of their being proportionate to the potency's faculty. Therefore, if the act of theological faith, considered in its species, is purely natural and thus proportionate to our intellect, it will be able to be elicited easily, without the requirement of a habit. **This is furthermore because** ease belongs to the same order as act and can be acquired by repeating an act. If, then, we can elicit the assent of faith by our natural powers, we will also be able to gain greater ease in this. But we cannot elicit [the act of faith] as is necessary. Therefore 'as necessary' does not define the manner as easy. **Finally, this is because** for an act to lead to salvation, it need not be done with ease. A sign of this is that even if it is done out of grace, it is usually done with difficulty. Therefore its being as it needs to be cannot consist [in its being done] in an easy manner.

Before we dive into the list delineated by *tum quia*, we can note a few other things. First, *ut vult Durandus* means that the Salamancan Carmelites are relating the opinion of William Durandus (ca. 1230–96). *Velle* when describing academic stances means 'to have an opinion.' Or, if you like, you can follow a similar English expression and say "as Durandus would have it."

---

[8] Salmanticenses, *Cursus theologicus*, tract. 19, *De gratia Dei*, disp. 3, dub. 3, § 2, n. 31.

Second, we note *ut constat*, which is a very common phrase. As in classical Latin, it frequently means 'as is established' or 'as is obvious.'

Third, the phrase *actus fidei Theologicae secundum suam speciem acceptus* is a prime example of two common usages. First, we see *accipere* meaning 'to take' in the sense of 'to consider' or 'to understand,' as when we say in English, "I am taking 'faith' here in the sense of a human act." Second, we have *secundum* meaning 'with reference to.' However, when we combine this with *secundum speciem*, nothing prevents translating this as 'in species' or 'specifically.' All it means is that we're talking about faith in terms of the *kind* of act it is (an intellectual one).

Fourth, you may have noticed the word *ly*. *Ly* can also be *li* or even *lu*. It is essentially the Scholastic attempt to make up for the fact that Latin doesn't have a definite article ('the'). Think of the French *le*. However, *ly* is not always to be translated as 'the.' Quite often, it is used to draw attention to a specific word or phrase, the kind of emphasis that we would create today by using italics or quotation marks. This is the case in the example above. One could also translate it by something like "the *expression* 'as necessary' … ."

Having made these observations, let's turn to the larger structure of the example. Repeating *tum quia* forms a list. Each element in that list is a supporting argument for the assertion made at the beginning. In effect, with the first *tum quia*, the Salamancan Carmelites are signaling from the start that a catalogue of supporting reasons for their position is about to follow, until we get to *tum denique quia* and learn that we have arrived at the last element in the list.

Back and Forth

One more thing to be aware of in Scholastic texts is that because they proceed in a *dialectic* manner, that is a back-and-forth style, it is essential that authors indicate which opinions are their own, which are their adversaries', and be able to give arguments and counter-arguments on both sides. To avoid getting lost in a lengthy discussion, we need to look for key words and phrases.

An author's own opinion will usually be stated clearly with *dico* ('I say') or *dicendum est* ('it should be said'). Objections may be given by *obiicitur* or simply implied by the structure. They may also be identified by phrases like *si dicatur* ('if it is said'). Replies to objections will either note the objection being responded to, as in *ad tertium dicendum quod* ('to the third objection, it should be said that') or with expressions like *evertitur* ('it is overturned'), *convellitur* ('it is demolished'), and so forth.

The proofs an author gives for his own position (*probationes*) may also enjoy multiple supporting arguments (*confirmationes*). Each of these may have objections and responses, which apply only to the *probatio* or *confirmatio* in question. We can see why it is important to keep the whole structure in mind and to read the full treatment of the question! Modern editions will usually help by clarifying the structure and emphasizing the author's own opinion.

CHAPTER IV
Sic Proceditur: The Passive and Impersonal Passive

Most of the Latin turns of phrase we will encounter in this guide have a straightforward English equivalent. For example, *inquantum* is 'inasmuch as'; and *fieri potest* is 'it is possible' (literally 'it can happen,' 'it can take place,' or 'it can be done'). However, Latin also has features that English does not. One of these, common to classical as well as Scholastic Latin, is reliance on the passive and particularly the impersonal passive.

The Simple Passive

Let's start with the simple passive voice. As you recall, the passive voice means that the subject is undergoing the action of the verb rather than being the agent driving that action. In English "He calls his sister" is active, whereas "He is being called by his sister" is passive.

Here is an example in Latin:

Praemittitur quod apud omnes est certum.[9]

Literal: What is certain to all **is laid out up front.**

Smooth: **We lay out up front** what everyone regards as certain.

Good English style often prefers the active voice, but Latin is much more open to using the passive. This means that in translation, we may sometimes want to change the voice, as the smoother example above illustrates. The missing agent is supplied in the smoother translation by inserting 'we.'

By the way, in the example above, note that *apud* in Latin can be used to indicate the thought of a person or group of people, their work, what they consider normal, etc., like *chez* in French. So, *apud Thomam* means 'according to Thomas,' 'in Thomas's thought,' or 'in the work of Thomas.' Interestingly, both *apud* and *chez* can also mean 'at the house of.'

The Impersonal Passive

In English, a verb can be passive if it is *transitive*, meaning that if it can take a direct object when it is active, then that object can be made into the subject of the sentence and the verb put into the passive. For example, "The dog bites the man" has a verb in the active voice ('bites'), one that is transitive

---

9   Jean-Baptiste Gonet, *Clypeus theologiae Thomisticae*, I, disp. 3, a. 5.

because we can specify what the dog is biting, in this case the man. This means that the verb can be made passive: "The man is bitten (by the dog)."

Latin is even more versatile. In Latin, even an *intransitive* verb can be made passive and put into what we call the impersonal passive. For example, in English "the man goes" is intransitive: No direct object is possible, and so there is no passive form of the verb 'to go.' In Latin, there is.

Probably the most famous example is from Virgil: *sic itur ad astra*.[10] How do we translate this into English? Well, Virgil is using the impersonal passive to make a general claim about how *anyone* might go to the stars. We have options for how to express this in English. We could say "this is how one goes to the stars." Or, we could use the informal 'you' (meaning anyone): "This is how you get to the stars." Or, we could use the first person plural: "This is how we get to the stars." Or, we could even change the whole thing around: "This is the path that leads to the stars."

The Scholastics use the impersonal passive *all the time*. For example, a Scholastic author might indicate the beginning of the first article of a question by saying *Ad primum sic proceditur* ('we proceed to the first article in this way'). Here, the English translation could safely omit this phrase. It exists really only for the sake of structure, and in a modern edition that structure is presented clearly with page layout, spacing, punctuation, and titles like "Article 1."

Other examples of the impersonal passive exist with the gerundive, as in *dicendum est* ('it should be said') or *distinguendum est* ('we must distinguish'). Again, these are ways of indicating a general necessity without having to specify who needs to do it. The implication is that the necessity is logical and, thus, that anyone taking up the question must proceed as the author intends.

---

10   *Aeneid* IX.641.

CHAPTER V
Obiter Dicta: **Indirect Discourse and Substantive Clauses**

It makes sense that Scholastic texts are filled with indirect discourse and substantive clauses. These are common enough in many texts, but Scholasticism is especially concerned with propositions and the right way to speak of things. In the course of examining, clarifying, impugning, and defending various viewpoints, indirect discourse occurs frequently.

Indirect Discourse

Whereas classical Latin favors the accusative with the infinitive for indirect statements, Scholastic Latin much more freely uses *quod, quia,* or *quoniam* with or without the subjunctive.

Consider the following:

Sic ergo **dicendum est, quod** in Deo **est** sapientia, bonitas, et hujusmodi, quorum quodlibet est ipsa divina essentia, et ita omnia sunt unum re.[11]	And so **it should be said that** in God **there is** wisdom, goodness, and other such things, each one of which is the divine essence itself. And thus they are all one in reality.
Est ergo **dicendum quod sit** una actio in Christo propter unum suppositum agens.[12]	Therefore **it should be said that there is** one action in Christ on account of the one suppositum acting.

By the way, *suppositum* means the individual thing, i.e., the stable, unified reality underlying all the possibly changing features or actions attributable to that individual. In the above example, the claim is that although Christ can act as God or as a man, he is only one agent who acts.

Substantive Clauses

Besides the accusative with the infinitive, Scholastic Latin makes heavy use of *quod, quia, quoniam,* and *ut* to deal with a whole phrase as if it were a single thing (a substantive clause). It can be helpful to mark off such phrases in English translation by an expression such as 'the fact that.'

---

11   Thomas Aquinas, *Super I Sent.*, d. 2, q. 1, a. 2, co.
12   Thomas Aquinas, *De unione Verbi incarnati*, a. 5, obj. 3.

For example:

Ex parte obiecti, **quod** finis sit ratio volendi media, ad perfectionem spectat.[13]	On the part of the object, **the fact that** the end is the reason for willing the means, pertains to its perfection.
	Or: On the part of the object, it pertains to perfection **that** the end be the reason for willing the means.
	Or: On the part of the object, **the end's being the reason** for willing the means belongs to its perfection.

Substantive clauses with *quod*, *quia*, *quoniam*, and *ut* also often involve pointer words like *hoc*, as in these examples:

Hoc non patiebatur status hominis viatoris, **quod** angelum per essentiam videret.[14]	*Literal:* The state of man as a wayfarer did not suffer **this**, [namely] **that** he would see an angel in its essence.
	Smooth: Man's state as a wayfarer **would not bear seeing** an angel in its essence.
Et quia Christus, inquantum est homo, **ad hoc** fuit praedestinatus et electus **ut** "esset praedestinatus Filius Dei in virtute sanctificationis," **hoc** fuit proprium sibi, **ut** haberet talem plenitudinem gratiae quod redundaret in omnes: secundum quod dicitur Ioan. I: "De plenitudine eius nos omnes accepimus."[15]	And because Christ as man was predestined and elected **to** "being the predestined Son of God in the power of sanctification" (Rom 1:4), it was proper to him **to** have a fullness of grace such as would overflow to all, according to what is said, "From his fullness we have all received" (Jn 1:16).

---

13   Francisco Suárez, *Disputationes in III Thomae*, disp. 5, sect. 1, q. 1, a. 4, n. 26.
14   Thomas Aquinas, *Summa theologiae* III, q. 30, a. 3, ad 1.
15   Thomas Aquinas, *Summa theologiae* III, q. 27, a. 5, ad 1.

Agilitas non solum pertinet ad motum, sed etiam ad sensum, et ad omnes alias operationes animae: ut **secundum hoc** dicatur corpus gloriosum esse agile, **quod** est perfecte habilitatum ad omnes operationes quae per corpus exercentur.[16]	Agility pertains not only to movement but also to the senses and to all the soul's other actions, so that a glorified body is said to be agile **with reference to the fact that** it is made completely fit for all the actions carried out through the body.
	Or: Agility pertains not only to movement but also to the senses and to all the soul's other actions, so that a glorified body is said to be agile **on the basis of its becoming** perfectly suited for all the actions carried out by the body.

We can see that pointer words (like *hoc*) usually disappear in translation because the clauses that are separated in Latin should be put together in English.

Substantive clauses also sometimes use the accusative with the infinitive, as in classical Latin:

Et **idem etiam videtur esse dicendum** de mansuetudine.[17]	And **it seems that the same should also be said** of meekness.

Sometimes constructions are combined in a way that facilitates clarity, especially when levels of indirectness overlap:

Videtur quod Deum esse non sit demonstrabile.[18]	It seems that it is not demonstrable that there is a God.
	Or: It seems that 'there is a God' is not demonstrable.
	Or: It seems that the fact that there is a God is not demonstrable.

16　Thomas Aquinas, *Super IV Sent.*, d. 49, q. 4, a. 5, ad 2.
17　Thomas Aquinas, *Summa theologiae* II-II, q. 170, a. 2, obj. 2.
18　Thomas Aquinas, *Summa theologiae* I, q. 2, a. 2, obj. 1.

While their style certainly differs from classical authors, the Scholastics employ the Latin language in a way suited to their purposes. Without the aid of advanced punctuation or typography, they distinguish indirect discourse as well as substantive clauses by using the constructions glimpsed in this chapter, especially *quod, quia, quoniam,* and *ut* as well as the accusative with the infinitive. A key lesson that emerges from all this is that we must read the entire sentence and be especially attentive to pointer words (like *hoc*) in order to untangle layers of indirect discourse and substantive clauses.

CHAPTER VI
Res Sic Se Habet: Some Peculiarities

It's obvious that Scholastic Latin differs greatly from Cicero. This makes sense, given that it served primarily a utilitarian purpose. Occasionally, we come across a beautiful or poetic turn of phrase, but for the most part, the beauty of Scholastic texts is to be found in the truths and images they convey. In addition to its more modern or functional style, Scholastic Latin also has some grammatical peculiarities. In this chapter, we will review five of the most common.

Not So Strict about the Subjunctive

It's true that classical authors don't always follow the rules when it comes to the subjunctive, but the Scholastics are even looser with it.

For example, here's a passage from Francesco Lychetus (1465–1520), the great commentator on John Duns Scotus (ca. 1266–1308), dealing with how angels pick out how much physical space to act upon:

Etsi angelus determinet sibi tantum locum, quod non maiorem, puta locum tricubitalem, **ita quod non possit** esse potestate sua in maiori loco; et similiter determinet sibi locum ita parvum, quod non minorem, puta locum digitalem, **ita quod potestate sua non possit** esse in minori loco, tamen se potest facere praesentem maiori et minori loco, accipiendo maius et minus infra spatium digitale et tricubitale, **ita quod potest** esse potestate sua in spatio bicubitali, et in spatio cubitali.[19]	Even if an angel determines for itself a space so large that it could not be larger (for example a space of three cubits) **such that by its power it cannot be** in a larger place, and likewise determines for itself a place so small that it could not be smaller (for example a space of one finger length) **such that by its power it cannot be** in a smaller place, it can still make itself present to a larger and smaller space, taking 'larger' and 'smaller' as meaning within the range of a finger-length space and that of three cubits, **such that by its power it can be** in a two-cubit space and a one-cubit space.

---

19 Francesco Lychetus, Commentary on John Duns Scotus, *In II Sent.*, d. 2, q. 6.

Leaving angels aside, notice that Lychetus uses the subjunctive for the first two result clauses and the indicative for the third. Perhaps it's because the first two have a greater feeling of counter-factuality in the context (what an angel could not do versus what it can do). Even so, we would expect the subjunctive in the third result clause, but we don't find it.

Comparative Adjectives in the Ablative End in -i

It's very common in Scholastic Latin for the ablative singular of comparative adjectives to end in -i rather than -e, as in classical Latin. To illustrate this, we can look at the same example from Lychetus cited above:

Etsi angelus determinet sibi tantum locum, quod non maiorem, puta locum tricubitalem, ita quod non possit esse potestate sua **in maiori loco**; et similiter determinet sibi locum ita parvum, quod non minorem, puta locum digitalem, ita quod potestate sua non possit esse **in minori loco**, tamen se potest facere praesentem maiori et minori loco, accipiendo maius et minus infra spatium digitale et tricubitale, ita quod potest esse potestate sua in spatio bicubitali, et in spatio cubitali.[20]	Even if an angel determines for itself a space so large that it could not be larger (for example a space of three cubits) such that by its power it cannot be **in a larger place**, and likewise determines for itself a place so small that it could not be smaller (for example a space of one finger length) such that by its power it cannot be **in a smaller place**, it can still make itself present to a larger and smaller space, taking 'larger' and 'smaller' as meaning within the range of a finger-length space and that of three cubits, such that by its power it can be in a two-cubit space and a one-cubit space.

The Gerund Often Takes the Place of the Gerundive

A gerund is the noun form of a verb. In English, the gerund often (confusingly) ends in -ing like many other forms. In classical Latin, the gerund is used when a verb needs to function as a noun in situations where the verb's infinitive is not appropriate. For example, 'one learns by reading' would be *legendo discitur*, where *legendo* is the ablative case of the gerund.

---

20 Francesco Lychetus, Commentary on John Duns Scotus, *In II Sent.*, d. 2, q. 6.

In classical Latin, to express purpose, an adjective derived from the gerund is often used. This adjective is called the gerundive because it comes from the gerund. For example, one way to say 'in order to read many pages' is *ad plurimas paginas legendas*. The adjective *legendas* qualifies the pages as 'needing to be read.'

In classical Latin, the gerund is sometimes used to express purpose, but the gerundive is more common. In Scholastic Latin, however, the situation is reversed. Scholastic Latin more commonly uses the gerund for purpose, though it does not exclude the gerundive. Further, when using the gerundive, classical Latin often puts the agent of the action (the one who is to perform it) in the dative case (the dative of agent). Scholastic Latin frequently (not always) uses the ablative of agent with the preposition *ab*.

For instance:

Utrum aliquis teneatur dimittere studium theologiae etiam si sit **aptus ad alios docendum**, ad hoc quod intendat saluti animarum?[21]	Whether one is bound to give up the study of theology to focus on the salvation of souls even if he is suited **to teach others**?
Prudentia et habitus ad cognitionem **rerum a nobis agendarum** pertinentes, sunt nobis magis naturales quam scientia aliarum rerum.[22]	Prudence and habits pertaining to knowledge of **matters we must tend to** are more natural to us than scientific knowledge of other things.
Unde hodie non licet de convenientia talis consuetudinis dubitare, aut illam in aliquo reprehendere: sed magis **curandum est Theologis** illam exponere atque tueri.[23]	Hence today it is not permissible to doubt about the appropriateness of this kind of custom or to criticize it in any respect. Rather, **theologians should take care** to explain and defend it instead.

---

21   Thomas Aquinas, *Quodlibet* I, q. 7 pr. 2.
22   Thomas Aquinas, *Super II Sent.*, d. 23, q. 2, a. 2, co.
23   Salmanticenses, *Cursus theologicus*, tract. 23, disp. 12, dub. 2, § 1, n. 9.

The Comparative Often Serves as the Superlative

Scholastics often use the comparative form of an adjective in place of the superlative. This means that the comparative form can frequently be translated by prefixing 'the most' in English or by using the superlative form. For example:

> Tertia ratio (et credo quod **melior** est) quia …[24]

> The third argument (and I believe it is **the best one**) is that …

Perfect Passive Participles in the Conjugation of Verbs Are Treated Like Adjectives

In later Latin, and thus in Scholastic Latin, perfect passive participles, normally used to form the passive forms of verbs in the perfect, pluperfect, and future perfect tenses, often get treated as simple adjectives. This leads the perfect, pluperfect, and future perfect forms of verbs to require the use of *esse* in these tenses. Thus, rather than *vocatus est* ('he was called'), as in classical Latin, Scholastics might say *vocatus fuit*.

For instance:

> Videtur quod beatus Matthaeus **non fuit vocatus** statim de teloneo ad statum apostolatus et perfectionis.[25]

> It seems that blessed Matthew **was not** immediately **called** from the customs post to the apostolic state and that of perfection.

The five peculiarities presented in this chapter are some of the most common in Scholastic texts. They generally will not pose much difficulty.

---

24   Thomas Aquinas, *Super I Sent.*, d. 13 q. 1 a. 3 ad 2.
25   Thomas Aquinas, *Quodlibet V*, q. 11, a. 1.

CHAPTER VII
Locutiones: Key Expressions

The examples in this guide have already exposed us to various turns of phrase commonly used by the Scholastics. Some of these turns of phrase are old expressions that became more common in Scholasticism, while others were unknown to the classical period. In this chapter, we will explain the most common turns of phrase needed for reading Scholastic Latin as well as a few words with special meanings in the context of academic debate. We will not worry about technical vocabulary, since terms of art in theology, philosophy, and the various natural sciences, require a dedicated lexicon in their own right. The meaning of technical terms can usually be found by having recourse to the resources listed in the resource list at the end of this guide.

The remainder of the present chapter consists of a list of the most important expressions arranged alphabetically. Learning these key expressions is a powerful way to get a handle on Scholastic Latin.

Accipere [or **sumere**]: Means generally 'to take' or 'to receive.' As in English, this can also include the sense of 'to understand in a certain way.'

Adverte etiam quod ly quasi **accipitur ut** est expressivum veritatis: non autem ut similitudinem importat.[26]	Note, also, that 'quasi' **is understood in the sense of** expressing a truth, not as implying likeness.

Adducere or **inducere**: The direct meaning of 'to introduce' or 'to bring in' includes the idea of citing something in an academic sense.

Et **inducit** Augustinum *contra Faustum* dicentem: …[27]	And he **cites** Augustine (*Against Faustus*), who says: …

Contingere [or **fieri**]: Often in the third person, it means that something occurs or happens.

However, it is usually best to translate the various forms of *contingit* as 'it is the case,' 'it can happen that,' or 'it is possible.'

---

26 Franciscus de Sylvestris Ferrariensis, *Commentarii in Summa contra gentiles* II, c. 23.
27 Francisco de Vitoria, *De legibus*, q. 90, a. 1.

Potentia rationalis perfecta per virtutem moralem, non est semper in suo actu, cum **non contingat** semper agere.²⁸	The rational power perfected by a moral virtue is not always in its act, since **it cannot** always be acting.
Contingit enim aliquod malum propter bonum velle; sicut qui vult furari, ut eleemosynas det.²⁹	For **it is possible** to will an evil for the sake of good, as when one wills to steal in order to give alms.

Dicere: Besides its usual meaning of 'to say,' *dicere* can be rendered 'to indicate,' 'to bespeak,' 'to call,' or 'to mean.'

Differentia nullam formam **dicit**, quae implicite in natura generis non contineatur.³⁰	A difference does not **indicate** any form not implicitly contained in the nature of the genus.
'Filius' solum **dicit** respectum ad Patrem, non ad creaturam.³¹	'Son' only **indicates** a respect to the Father, not a creature.
Et ne fiat contentio de nomine univocationis, univocum conceptum **dico**, qui ita est unus quod eius unitas sufficit ad contradictionem, affirmando et negando ipsum de eodem.³²	And lest there be contention over the term 'univocity,' **what I mean** by a univocal concept is a concept that is one in such a way that its unity suffices for there to be a contradiction in affirming and denying it of the same thing.

Est with the infinitive of a verb: When *est* is used with the infinitive X, the sense is usually that 'one can do X,' or 'we can do X.'

For example, in the midst of explaining his First Way of proving that God exists (the argument from motion), Aquinas says:

---

28 Thomas Aquinas, *Super II Sent.*, d. 27, q. 1, a. 1, obj. 3.
29 Thomas Aquinas, *Super II Sent.*, d. 38, q. 1, a. 5, obj. 1.
30 Thomas Aquinas, *Super II Sent.*, d. 3, q. 1, a. 6, ad 1.
31 Bonaventure, *Super III Sent.*, d. 1, a. 1, q. 4, obj. 4.
32 John Duns Scotus, *Ordinatio I*, d. 3, pars 1, q. 2, n. 26.

Omne ergo quod movetur, oportet ab alio moveri. Si ergo id a quo movetur, moveatur, oportet et ipsum ab alio moveri et illud ab alio. Hic autem **non est procedere** in infinitum.³³	Therefore, whatever is moved must be moved by something else. If, then, the thing by which it is moved is moved, then it, too, must itself be moved by something else and that by something else in turn. But here **we cannot proceed** to infinity.

Habere: Various constructions involving *habere* are often better paraphrased in English.

For example, *habere + de* or *habere aliquid de* refers to how much something possesses a certain quality:

Inter omnia peccata minimum est originale, eo quod **minimum habet de voluntario**.³⁴	Among all sins, original sin is the least by virtue of the fact that **it is least characterized by voluntariness**.

Similarly, *habere hoc quod* (a pointer word with a substantive clause, as we saw in chapter 5) or *habere* with the infinitive of a verb can express what is proper to something.

Constat quod voluntas divina **hoc naturaliter habet quod** peccare non potest.³⁵	It is obvious that the divine will **naturally has the property of** being unable to sin. *Or*: It is obvious that the divine will **naturally possesses** the inability to sin. *Or*: It is obvious that the divine will **has a natural inability** to sin.

---

33 Thomas Aquinas, *Summa theologiae* I, q. 2, a. 3, co.
34 Thomas Aquinas, *Super II Sent.*, d. 33, q. 2, a. 1, ad 2.
35 Thomas Aquinas, *Super II Sent.*, d. 23, q. 1, a. 1, obj. 4.

Licet voluntas elevetur et iuvetur per aliquid supernaturale, non tamen sequitur quod non sit libera; quia cum Deus operetur omnia in omnibus, etiam ipsa inclinatio et elevatio voluntatis est a Deo ex quo non tollitur libertas voluntatis, quia solus **habet immittere** in voluntatem.[36]	Although the will is elevated and helped by something supernatural, it does not follow that it is not free. For, because God works all things in all, even the very inclination and elevation of the will is from God, whereby the will's freedom is not taken away, since he alone **has the power to introduce a direction into** the will.

Habere with the infinitive X can also mean 'to have to X' in the sense of necessity, as it does in English:

Si ponamus Spiritum Sanctum non esse, **haberemus dicere** quod in Deo non esset dilectio nisi essentialis.[37]	If we posit that the Holy Spirit does not exist, then **we would have to say** that in God there is no love but that of his essence.

Incidere in idem or **coincidere in idem**: Literally, 'to come to the same thing,' but more straightforwardly means 'to be identical.'

Causa et effectus **non incidunt in idem**.[38]	Cause and effect **are not identical**.

Instantia, -ae: A 'counter-example.' This makes sense given that a counter-example is one that *stands against* a given opinion. Be careful not to confuse *instantia, -ae* with *instans, -ntis* (an 'instant').

Sed ista **instantia** nulla est.[39]	But this **counter-example** is null. Or: But this **counter-example** amounts to nothing.

---

36   Thomas Aquinas, *Lectura Romana in I Sent.*, d. 17, q. 1, a. 1, ad 4.
37   Denys the Carthusian, *In I Sent.*, d. 14, qc. 6.
38   Thomas Aquinas, *Super II Sent.*, d. 36, q. 1, a. 3, obj. 2.
39   Thomas Aquinas, *Super I Sent.*, d. 38, q. 1, a. 5, ad 4.

Inquantum: By itself, just as in English it means 'inasmuch as.' This is a functional equivalent of *secundum quod* (see below).

However, it is often advisable to paraphrase longer expressions containing *inquantum*, such as *inquantum huiusmodi*, *X inquantum X*, or *X inquantum Y*. Such expressions are intended to focus our consideration on a particular feature of a given thing:

Omne quod movetur, **inquantum huiusmodi**, est in potentia.[40]	Everything that is moved is, **considered in this respect**, in potency.
Si enim **homo inquantum homo** esset albus, albedo necessario inesset homini.[41]	For if man **precisely as man** were white, then whiteness would be in man necessarily.

Littera, -ae: Besides 'letter,' it can meant the 'text' that a particular author is commenting on or working from.

Solutis quaestionibus ad **litteram** redeamus.[42]	Having solved these questions, let's get back to the **text**.
Hoc idem videtur ex definitione Augustini inducta in **littera**.[43]	We see the same on the basis of Augustine's definition cited in the **text**.

Ly (also **li** or **lu**): Serves as a direct article ('the'), which standard Latin lacks. *Ly* is sometimes used for emphasis, as when Aquinas explains why John's Gospel begins by referring to '*the* Word':

Ut ergo Evangelista hanc supereminentiam divini Verbi significaret, ipsum Verbum absque ulla additione nobis absolute proposuit;	Therefore, in order to signify this surpassing eminence of the divine Word, the evangelist has proposed the Word to us absolutely and without any addition.

---

40 Thomas Aquinas, *Contra gentiles* I, c. 13.
41 John Duns Scotus, *Quaestiones de lib. I Sent.*, d. 2, q. 7, n. 165.
42 Peter Abelard, *Logica nostrorum petitioni sociorum*.
43 Thomas Aquinas, *Super I Sent.*, d. 1, q. 1, a. 1, obj. 9.

et quia Graeci, quando volunt significare aliquid segregatum et elevatum ab omnibus aliis, consueverunt apponere articulum nomini, per quod illud significatur—sicut Platonici volentes significare substantias separatas, puta bonum separatum, vel hominem separatum, vocabant illud **ly** per se bonum, vel **ly** per se hominem—ideo Evangelista volens significare segregationem et elevationem istius Verbi super omnia, apposuit articulum ad hoc nomen logos, ut si dicatur in Latino, **ly** verbum.[44]	And because the Greeks, when they wish to signify something separate and elevated beyond everything else usually affix an article to the term whereby it is signified—as the Platonists, when they want to signify the separated substances, for example separated good or separated man, called them '*the* good as such' or '*the* man as such'—thus the Evangelist, when he wanted to signify the separation and elevation of this Word above all things, affixed an article to the term 'logos', as if we were to say in Latin, '*the* word.'

More often, however, and especially when dealing with grammar and logic, *ly* indicates that a term or word is being discussed precisely as a term or word. In such cases, it is often better to use quotation marks or italics rather than attempt to translate *ly* directly.

For example, when dealing with the different kinds of "supposition" (how the same word can have different referents depending on context), Ralph Strode (fl. ca. 1350) says this:

Ly currit supponit ibi in ista propositione: **Ly** currit est verbum materialiter.[45]	In the proposition 'runs is a word,' 'runs' exercises material supposition.

Material supposition means that in the context of the sentence 'runs is a word' the word 'runs' is referring to itself precisely as a word and not to

---

44 Thomas Aquinas, *Super Ioannem*, c. 1, l. 1.
45 Ralph Strode, *De Suppositione materiali*, in Albert of Saxony, *Albert of Saxony's Twenty-Five Disputed Questions on Logic: A Critical Edition of His Quaestiones Circa Logicam*, ed. Michael J. Fitzgerald, Studien und Texte zur Geistesgeschichte des Mittelalters 79 (Leiden: Brill, 2002), Appendix 1.

anyone actually running in the real world. Since they lacked quotation marks and italics, we can see why the Scholastics had recourse to words like *ly* in order to delineate such meta-discussions about language! And, lest we think that we can leave such matters to grammarians and logicians, we should bear in mind that discussions of this sort also pop up throughout philosophical and theological works.

Motivum, -i: 'Motive,' but also 'argument,' 'rationale,' or 'line of reasoning.'

Refertur opinio contraria, et convelluntur aliqua eius **motiva**.[46]	We relate the contrary opinion and overturn some of its **supporting arguments**.

Natum est: Literally meaning 'was born,' *natum est* is used with an expression of purpose (such as the infinitive of a verb) to state that something acts in a certain way by its nature or is meant to act in a certain way.

Quod eodem modo se habet nunc et prius **natum est** consimiles operationes efficere.[47]	What exists in the same way now and previously **is meant** to carry out actions similar to one another.
Tunc aliqua virtus cogitur, quando ad oppositum suae inclinationis movetur; sed liberum arbitrium, eo ipso quod liberum, ita **natum est** inclinari ad unum oppositum sicut et ad reliquum.[48]	A power is compelled when it is moved to the opposite of its inclination. But free will, by the very fact that it is free, **is naturally apt** to be inclined to one opposing side just as to the remaining side.

Oportet: Very common and usually best translated by 'must' or 'need.'

Oportet perfectionem perfectibili proportionatam esse.[49]	A perfection **must** be proportionate to what can be [so] perfected.

---

46 Salmanticenses, *Cursus theologicus*, tract. 21, disp. 2, dub. 1, § 7.
47 Bonaventure, *Super III Sent.*, d. 18, a. 1, q. 2, sc 5.
48 Bonaventure, *Super II Sent.*, d. 25, p. 2, a. 1, q. 5, sc 5.
49 Thomas Aquinas, *Super II Sent.*, d. 30, q. 1, a. 1, s.c. 2.

Cum Deus sit ens per essentiam, **oportet** quod sit causa omnis rei habentis esse participatum.⁵⁰	Since God is being essentially, he **must** be the cause of each thing that possesses participated being.
Quomodo autem maior est unio voluntatis cum volito quam intellectus cum intellecto, alibi satis declaravi, **nec oportet** repetere, quia nihil novi audivi in contrarium nisi iam tacta.⁵¹	Now as to how the union of the will with what it wills is greater than the union of the intellect with what it understands, I have stated this clearly enough elsewhere, **and there is no need** to repeat it, since I have not heard anything new favoring the contrary view, except what I have already touched on.

Propositum, -i: In addition to the normal meanings of 'plan,' 'proposal,' 'resolution,' etc., it can mean the specific issue under discussion.

Unde obiectio nihil probat ad **propositum**.⁵²	Hence the objection proves nothing regarding **the point at issue**.

Pro tanto: Basically 'on this account.' As with *hoc … quod* and similar expressions, it can rely on an entire substantive clause as its explanatory basis.

Pro tanto dicuntur voluisse sine labore gloriam consequi, **quia** propria virtute assequi voluerunt.⁵³	[The fallen angels] are said to have wished to achieve glory without effort **on account of the fact** that they wanted to attain it by their own power.

Puta (also **ut puta** or **puta si**): 'For example' or 'suppose.'

---

50 Jean Capréolus, *Defensiones divi Thomae in I Sent.*, d. 3, q. 1, rat. 4, ad 1 inst.
51 Henry of Ghent, *Quodlibet X*, q. 15, sol.
52 Thomas Aquinas, *Super II Sent.*, d. 28, q. 1, a. 4, ad 5.
53 Thomas Aquinas, *Super II Sent.*, d. 5, q. 1, a. 3, ad 3.

Quaedam ignoranter aguntur, et sine tristitia, **puta si** aliquis occidit hostem quem quaerit occidere, putans occidere cervum.[54]	Some things are done out of ignorance and yet without sorrow. **For example, if** someone kills a man—whom he actually is seeking to kill—when he thinks that he is killing a deer instead.

Quantum ad: 'As regards' or 'in regard to.' As part of a larger expression, however, such as *quantum ad se*, a paraphrase might be better. Sometimes a simple 'in' does the trick more elegantly.

Animam facit gratam et **quantum ad** se et **quantum ad** eius potentias.[55]	[Grace] makes the soul pleasing both **in** itself and **in** its powers.

Secundum quod: Usually 'insofar as,' 'to the extent that,' 'according as,' or simply 'as.' *Secundum quod* must not be confused with *secundum quid* (a technical term meaning 'in a certain respect'). *Secundum quod* is a functional equivalent of *inquantum* (see above).

It is often advisable to paraphrase longer expressions containing *secundum quod*, such as *secundum quod huiusmodi*, *X secundum quod X*, or *X secundum quod Y*. Such expressions are intended to focus our consideration of a thing on a specific aspect of it:

Deus in satisfactione non quaerit recompensationem de genere humano, **secundum quod est** in statu peccati, sed **secundum quod fuisset**, si non peccasset.[56]	What God is seeking in satisfaction is recompense from the human race, not **as it does exist**, in the state of sin, but instead **as it would have existed** if it had not sinned.
Quoddam namque donum est a Spiritu sancto, sed non cum Spiritu sancto, quia praeparat ad Spiritum sanctum;	For there is a gift that is from the Holy Spirit but not with the Holy Spirit because it prepares for the Holy Spirit.

---

54 Thomas Aquinas, *Summa theologiae* I-II, q. 6, a. 8, obj. 3.
55 Bonaventure, *Super III Sent.*, d. 36, a. 1, q. 1, resp.
56 Bonaventure, *Super III Sent.*, d. 20, a. 1, q. 3, ad 4.

et tale donum est **timor servilis secundum quod huiusmodi**.[57]	And this kind of gift is **servile fear precisely as servile**.
Et ideo magis est haec vera, Christus, **secundum quod iste homo**, est Deus, quam ista, Christus, **secundum quod homo**, est Deus.[58]	And thus this [proposition], 'Christ **as this man** is God' is more true than this one, 'Christ **as man** is God.'

Velle: Besides meaning 'to will' or 'to wish,' in an academic context, *velle* also has the sense of 'to be of the opinion' or 'to understand in a certain way.' More colloquially, a phrase like *ut vult Durandus* could be translated 'as Durandus would have it.'

Item, 'incarnari' non est aliud quam 'in carnem mitti,' sicut **vult** Augustinus; sed impossibile est, Patrem mitti, cum non habeat alium, a quo sit: ergo impossibile est Patrem incarnari.[59]	Again, 'to become incarnate' is nothing other than 'to be sent in the flesh,' as Augustine **understands it**. But it is impossible for the Father to be sent, since he has no one from whom he is. Therefore it is impossible for the Father to become incarnate.

---

57 Bonaventure, *Super III Sent.*, d. 34, a. 1, q. 1, ad 1.
58 Thomas Aquinas, *Summa theologiae* III, q. 16, a. 11, ad 3.
59 Bonaventure, *Super III Sent.*, d. 1, a. 1, q. 4, sc 2.

CHAPTER VIII
Non Habet Locum: Foreign Influences, Calques, and Technical Terms

The rise of Scholasticism is contemporaneous with the recovery of lost Greek texts and new Arabic texts, especially the works of Aristotle and engagements with them. Because these works were translated—sometimes more than once—into Latin, Scholastic Latin is often filled with individual words and phrases that are attempts to render foreign ideas and expressions (calques). If we are not attentive to this, our reading will distort the author's intention. Actually, we should also keep in mind that the Scholastic author in question may be misunderstanding the author he himself is employing due to a misleading or faulty Latin translation.

All this means that we will come across Latin words or phrases that have a technical meaning, sometimes rooted in the foreign origin of an expression. For example, when addressing an argument that the world has always existed because plant and animal species tend to reproduce themselves indefinitely, Aquinas says:

> Unde **locum non habet** haec ratio ...[60]   Hence this argument **is baseless** ...

It may seem as if Aquinas is simply claiming that there's no 'place' (*locus*) for the proposed argument. The problem he sees with the argument's reasoning, after all, is that it presupposes the existence of plant and animal species. Thus, it's one thing to acknowledge that they tend to reproduce themselves to eternity but quite another to conclude from this that they must have existed from all eternity.

However, this is a case where the word *locus* connotes more than just 'place.' Here *locus* is the Latin version of the Greek τόπος, which features in a work of Aristotle's called the *Topics*. In this work, Aristotle outlines various schemes, sources, or patterns for argumentation called τόποι. In Latin the literal translation of τόπος, i.e., *locus*, became common through Cicero and Boethius. Thus, we should understand Aquinas's claim more precisely as the rejection of a specific template for valid argumentation.

In other words, what he's saying is that the topical rule of argumentation that we can argue from one case to a parallel case doesn't apply because the fact that plant and animal species tend to perpetuate themselves forever into the *future* doesn't mean that they have always existed going back forever in the *past*. Their tendency to perpetuate themselves presupposes that they exist, and whether these species have always existed is precisely what needs to be demonstrated. Thus he rejects the argument as lacking a valid logical *locus*.

---

[60]   Thomas Aquinas, *Summa contra gentiles* II, c. 36, n. 5.

In other instances, a phrase may stand out more obviously as a calque than *locus* does. For example:

Licet anima humana non habeat materiam partem sui, est tamen forma corporis; et ideo **quod quid erat esse** suum, includit habitudinem ad corpus.[61]	Although the human soul does not have matter as part of it, it is still the form of the body. And thus its **what-it-was-meant-to-be** includes a connection to the body.

Here the Latin *quod quid erat esse*—again quite literally—translates the Greek τὸ τί ἦν εἶναι from Aristotle's *Metaphysics*. The phrase even acts as a noun (qualified by *suum* in the example above). Hence a good way to translate it is 'what-it-was-to-be' or 'what-it-was-meant-to-be,' which basically amounts to the essence or genuine, full-fledged being of a thing. In the example above, what Aquinas is saying is that the human soul is only fully itself when its intrinsic relationship to the body is included.

Another example of a single-word calque in Latin, is the noun *intentio* and the adjective *intentionalis*, translating the Arabic *ma'nâ*, which means something like 'concept' or 'mental expression.' Without this background knowledge, we would easily misunderstand the affirmation:

Esse naturale praecedit esse **intentionale**.[62]	Natural existence precedes **conceptual** existence.

When reading Scholastic texts, we should always be on the lookout for attempts to render foreign expressions in Latin.

The Scholastics also did not hesitate to coin new words as needed, especially to add levels of abstraction to their discussions. For example, they developed words like *quidditas* ('what-ness'), *anitas* ('whether-ness'), *haecceitas* ('this-ness'), and *perseitas* ('on-its-own-ness').

Further, they used many Latin words and phrases endowed with technical meanings. Two of the most common are *simpliciter* and *secundum quid*. In Scholastic discourse, *simpliciter* means 'in the straightforward sense' or 'without qualification.' In other words, it refers to the natural, direct way of taking something. In contrast, *secundum quid* means 'in a certain respect' or 'in a qualified sense.' It comes from *secundum* + *(ali)quid*, which is literally

---

61 Thomas Aquinas, *Quaestio disputata de Anima*, a. 3, ad 20.
62 Thomas Aquinas, *Super IV Sent.*, d. 44, q. 2, a. 1, qc. 3, ad 2.

'with reference to a given thing.' By the way, *ali-* drops off from forms of *aliquid* more often than in classical Latin.

Finally, we should note that a particular class of technical expressions to watch out for is those pertaining to logic. We have already seen *locus* above. Other common words include *consequentia* (the logical 'entailment' leading from premise to conclusion), *sequela* (an 'inference'), and *antecedens* (the 'antecedent' or first half of a proposition of the form 'if A, then B'). Sometimes, entire phrases having a technical meaning in logic appear, such as *de primo ad ultimum*, which is literally 'from the first to the last,' but actually refers to a logical rule sometimes called the 'chain rule,' meaning that starting from 'if A, then B; and, if B, then C,' we can conclude to 'if A, then C.'

A good lexicon, such as one of those included in this guide's resource list, helps in deciphering such technical terms.

CHAPTER IX
Caeteris Deficientibus: When All Else Fails

So what about when we find ourselves at our wits' end, with little or no idea of what a given text means? Here are six strategies for how to proceed.

Strategy 1: Search within the Text

One of the first things to try, if you have a digital copy of the text, is to search for the expression that is puzzling you within the same text. You may find another passage where the author uses the expression again in a way where context will help you discern its meaning, or even a passage where the author defines it for you.

If you don't have a digital copy of the text, try searching on Google Books with the author's name and the troubling expression (both with and without quotation marks). Be careful, too, to try variations on word endings if needed. For example, search for *vocatus* as well as *vocatos* and *vocatis*.

Strategy 2: Google Book Search or Google Web Search

Another thing to try is a search of Google Books in general or even a web search, leaving out any author information. There may be another Scholastic author who uses the expression in a clearer way, or you may find a dictionary or modern scholarly work that explains it. You may even find an English translation of another text containing the expression. At a minimum, you'll gain a rough idea of how common the troubling expression is and what kinds of works it appears in.

Strategy 3: Topical Web Search

If searching for variations on the expression itself doesn't help, scrutinize the context and figure out what topics it must relate to. For example, if you know it's an example drawn from botany or astronomy, or if you know it's a text dealing with providence and predestination, you might want to do a general web search for the author's view of these matters. Someone may have written an article or a book dealing with the subject, and learning about your author's opinion on that subject may give you enough information to figure out the expression.

Strategy 4: Use the Resource List

Some of the resources listed at the end of this guide can be found online; others cannot. In any case, they are worth combing through using the context you can glean from the text you're working with. If you can't find the precise expression, you can also read up on the relevant topic, as in Strategy 3 above.

Strategy 5: Phone a Friend

You probably thought of this already, but it's worth mentioning: Don't forget to ask for help if you need it. Call a friend. Email an expert, such as the translator or editor of a related text. Post in an online forum. It never hurts to ask. Someone else with very specialized knowledge may enjoy the opportunity to share it with you.

Strategy 6: Stay the Course

When you absolutely cannot make any headway in understanding an expression or even a whole passage, just skip it. You never know what context you may discover later in the text that will give you the clue you need or obviate the need to read the passage in the first place.

CHAPTER X
Sample Text I

In this text, the Salmanticenses address the question of whether more than one priest can consecrate the same host. A bit of background: In the Catholic Church today, it is normal for multiple priests to "concelebrate" the Mass, i.e., to say the words of consecration together over the same bread (the host) and wine. In the seventeenth century, when the Salmanticenses were writing, the only concelebration that took place was at the ordination of priests (or of a bishop), when all the newly ordained would say the words of consecration over the host together with the bishop who had just ordained them. Whether this was a true concelebration (with all those saying the words actually consecrating the same host together) or only for the sake of ceremony or instruction was a debated point.

The original text is on the left, with occasional notes to assist the reader on the right.

DUBIUM II[63]

Utrum plures sacerdotes possint eandem hostiam consecrare?

Multis modis intelligi potest, quod plures sacerdotes concurrant ad unius hostiae consecrationem.	A "doubt" is a question to be addressed.
Primo si unus intendat consecrare unam partem hostiae, et alter alteram. Et quidem si quilibet intendat consecrare hostiae partem, sed illam non determinet, sed in confuso procedat; minime consecrabit:	**First Sense.**
quia forma consecrationis est demonstrativa, et designans materiam determinatam, ut diximus disp. 4. dub. 6. Si autem eorum unus intendat consecrare unam determinate partem, quam assignaret intentione, aut etiam signo externo, et alius similiter aliam, ut contingeret hostiae partes distinguendo penicillo: tunc quilibet partem a se designatam consecrabit: quia concurrunt omnia, quae pro valore consecrationis desiderantur.	In Aristotle's understanding, form is what determines and matter is what is determined. Form and matter together combine to form the individual thing. *Valor* here means 'validity.'

---

63 From the Salmanticenses, *Cursus theologicus*, tract. 23, disp. 12, dub. 2.

Secundo intelligi potest, quod ex omnibus ad consecrandum concurrentibus singuli intendant totam adaequate hostiam consecrare. Quod adhuc bifariam contingere posset. Nam et posset

quilibet intendere consecrare non absolute, sed dependenter a consecratione alterius tanquam a conditione, ut si Petrus diceret, *Volo consecrare, si Ioannes consecret*: in quo casu unaquaeque consecratio foret conditionalis, et ab altera dependens. Sed in tali casu non solum intentio esset peccaminosa, sed et inutilis, et minime conficeret sacramentum: quippe ad huius valorem requiritur intentio absoluta, ut generaliter statuimus tract. praeced. disp. 7, dub. 2. Posset etiam fieri, quod quilibet consecrantium haberet intentionem absolutam, et totalem consecrandi. Et in hoc sensu procedit istius dubii difficultas.

Second Sense.

Sub-Distinction.

Absolute: 'unconditionally.'

In hoc sensu procedit: This clarifies the scope of the question from this point forward.

§ UNICUS

Defenditur, et explicatur communis sententia.

7. Dicendum est plures sacerdotes posse eamdem hostiam consecrare. Ita Div. Thomas in praesenti art. 2, in 4, distinctione 13, questione 1, art. 2, questiunc. 2, cui subscribunt ita unanimiter omnes Theologi, ut opus non sit aliquos in particulari referre.

Dicendum est: The authors' own opinion.

Divus: Another way of saying 'Saint.'

In praesenti: In this case, Aquinas's commentary on Peter Lombard's *Sentences*.

Probatur primo: quia concurrentibus multis sacerdotibus ad consecrandum unam, et eamdem hostiam cum intentione immediate explicata, concurrunt omnia requisita ad valorem consecrationis: ergo in tali casu una, et eadem hostia ab omnibus illis consecratur. Antecedens patet: quia datur materia apta, et sufficienter praesens, ut supponitur: deinde forma: praeterea intentio, cum quilibet sacerdos habeat intentionem totalem, et absolutam consecrandi illam materiam: nihil autem praeter haec desiderari valet ad sacramenti, et consecrationis valorem. Confirmatur: quia quilibet eorum sacerdotum, si seorsim concurreret, consecraret: ergo etiam simul concurrens consecrat: atque ideo et omnes. Nec enim est maior ratio, ut unus potius consecret, quam alius: nec motivum, ut nullus consecret. Si dicatur consecrationem non fieri nisi in ultimo instanti prolationis verborum, iuxta doctrinam traditam tract. praeced. disput. 4, dub. 5, et fieri non posse, ut verba consecrationis prolata a multis sacerdotibus in eodem temporis instanti terminentur. Id, inquam, si dicatur facile evertitur: quia nulla est repugnantia in eo, quod prolationes verborum finiantur in eodem momento. Quin nullum est instans, in quo non multa fiant, et terminentur, utputa hominum nativitates, mortes, negotia. Quare itaque repugnabit plures locutiones eodem momento finiri?

First Proof.

Proof of the Antecedent. *Datur* here means 'there is.'

Supporting Proof of the Antecedent.

Objection.

Reply to the Objection.

Si ulterius dicatur implicare, quod idem effectus proveniat simul a multis causis, et subinde quod eadem transsubstantiatio fiat simul a multis sacerdotibus, id iam reiectum, et superatum relinquitur supra disputatione 2, dub. ult. nu. 68, quin opus hic eam difficultatem diluere.

Further Objection.
Implicare: To contain a logical contradiction.

Diluere: To resolve.

8. Probatur secundo: quia quando sacerdotes ordinantur, omnes simul cum Episcopo ordinante proferunt verba consecrationis: quod vanum esset, nisi possent simul cum Episcopo eamdem hostiam consecrare: fieri itaque valet, ut una, et eadem hostia a multis sacerdotibus consecretur. Confirmatur: quia cum aliquis consecratur Episcopus, quatuor Episcopi, nempe tres consecrantes, et unus consecratus, simul consecrant eamdem hostiam, et conficiunt unum numero sacramentum: ergo idem quod prius. Quamvis enim hic posterior casus sit facilior, quam in argumento propositus; siquidem Episcopi concurrentes sunt sapientiores, et possunt ad hoc tendere, ut simul finiant consecrationis verba in eodem instanti; quod non ita facile continget in plurimis sacerdotibus recenter ordinatis, qui simul concurrere solent: id tamen minime refert: tum quia ipso exemplo plurium sacerdotum simul consecrantium probatur immediate nostra conclusio, nempe plures sacerdotes posse unam, et eamdem hostiam consecrare. Tum quia hoc exemplo prior plurimorum sacerdotum recenter ordinatorum

Second Proof.

Supporting Proof.

Unum numero: Numerical unity is one kind of unity. If A and B are numerically identical, then they are the self-same individual being, not only two of the same kind of being.

Sapientiores: Here, 'more experienced.'

List of Reasons.

casus facilior, et verisimilior redditur: nam si quatuor Episcopi possunt verba consecrationis simul in eodem momento finire; non repugnat quod plures, quam quatuor, eodem modo consecrent simul in eodem instanti verba absolvendo.

Dissimulare tamen non debemus utriusque exempli, et praesertim primi difficultatem: quia licet nemo neget, quod si plures sacerdotes simul concurrant ad consecrationem unius hostiae, et simul finiant consecrationis verba in eodem momento, omnes consecrabunt: et similiter nemo neget possibile esse metaphysice loquendo, et per respectum ad divinam potentiam, quod omnes simul finiant verba in eodem instanti: nihilominus in consecratione plurium sacerdotum ordinatorum id est moraliter impossibile. Nam difficillimum est fieri tantam adunationem vocum, et syllabarum tum consecrantium cum Episcopo, tum ipsorum sacerdotum inter se, ut omnes simul per idem indivisibile temporis terminentur: quin experimento patet rem aliter contingere, aliis prius incipientibus, et aliis post alios prolationem terminantibus. Unde consequenter fit hoc exemplum non satis convenienter expendi pro nostrae, et communis assertionis confirmatione: quippe usus ille plurimis inconvenientibus expositus est: atque ideo minime probandus videtur. Si enim unus ex sacerdotibus consecrantibus Episcopum praevenit, sequitur Episcopum non consecrare, quippe cuius verba reperiunt materiam

Explanation.

Dissimulare ... non debemus: The authors acknowledge that the real difficulty is a practical one, not a logical one.

Moraliter impossibile: Something is 'morally' impossible if it is impossible in terms of reasonable human action.

It is considered sacrilegious for a priest to attempt to consecrate something that cannot be consecrated (like a host that has already been consecrated).

praeconsecratam: si autem Episcopus praeveniat, caeteri consecrare non valent. Unde et Episcopus, et alii exponuntur periculo proferendi verba consecrationis super materiam indebitam, atque ideo et graviter peccandi: sicut plane peccaret, qui advertens hostiam esse ab alio consecratam, consecrare illam tentaret. Deinde sic agendo contingens est, quod non omnes consecrent utramque speciem: sed solus Episcopus consecret hostiam, si alios praeveniat; et alii e contra consecrent calicem, si praeveniant Episcopum: unde consequenter eveniet, quod nemo eorum faciat, et offerat perfectum sacrificium. Unde Durandus in 4, dist. 13, quaest. 3, nu. 10, suffragantibus Angelo, et Gabriele censet hanc consuetudinem esse periculosam, et merito abolendam. Pauludanus autem eodem loco, quaest. 4, Caietanus in praes. artic 2, dubitant de convenientia talis consuetudinis. Richardus denique dist. cit. art. 2, quest. 1, et quidam alii sentiunt in tali casu solum Episcopum consecrare, sacerdotes vero recenter ordinatos non consecrare, sed proferre verba consecrationis mere recitative, et materialiter, instructionis gratia. Sicut etiam quilibet eorum dicit, *Calicem salutaris accipiam etc. et sanguis, quam potavi*: et tamen nemo illorum calicem sumit.

In order to offer a complete Mass, the priest celebrating the Mass must himself consecrate both bread and wine.

9. Verum enimvero quamvis haec res olim non fuerit adeo certa; hodie tamen minime potest in dubium revocari.

Primum liquet: tum quia olim haec consuetudo non erat universalis in tota Ecclesia catholica, sed solum in aliquibus Ecclesiis observabatur, ut satis evidenter significat D. Thomas in praes. artic. 2, in *Sed contra* dicens: « Secundum consuetidinem quarumdam Ecclesiarum sacerdotes, cum de novo ordinantur, concelebrant Episcopo ordinanti. » Nulla autem consuetudo particularium Ecclesiarum praestat efficax argumentum, sed sola consuetudo universalis Ecclesiae. Tum etiam quia ipsum antiquum Pontificale Romanum innuebat sacerdotes recenter ordinatos non celebrare, nec consecrare, cum disponebat: « Dicant omnia, quae sunt in Missali, sicut si celebrarent » Unde vetustiores Scholastici potuerant de convenientia huius consuetudinis dubitare, illam magis, aut minus probantes. Secundum etiam constat propter opposita motiva: quia modo universalis Ecclesia Romana habet hanc consuetudinem in ordinatione sacerdotum. Et Pontificale Romanum novum aperte significat omnes sacerdotes cum Episcopo ordinante celebrare, et consecrare, cum disponit: « Curet Pontifex, ut morose, et alte canonem dicat. » Et rursus: « Eodem momento debent ab ordinatis verba consecrationis dici, quo dicuntur ab Episcopo. » Superflua autem foret tanta cura, si omnes simul non celebrarent, et consecrarent. Unde hodie non licet de convenientia talis consuetudinis dubitare, aut illam in aliquo reprehendere: sed

First Reason.

The *Pontificale Romanum* is the liturgical book with the instructions for the ordination Mass.

Second Reason.

magis curandum est Theologis illam exponere atque tueri.

Quod diversimodo explicant, licet omnes conveniant in eo, quod cuncti consecrantes debeant suam intentionem ad idem instans consecrationis referre, ut docent Innocentius Tertius lib. 4, *de mysterio altaris*, cap. 25, et D. Thomas in hoc artic. 2, ubi ait: « Nec propter hoc iteratur consecratio, quia sicut Innocentius Tertius dicit, omnium intentio debet ferri ad idem instans consecrationis. » Et quidem Martinus de Ledesma, Valentia, et quidam alii dicunt referendam esse intentionem usque ad ultimum instans eius, qui ex omnibus consecrantibus ultimus verba profert. Sed Paludanus docet referri debere ad ultimum instans, in quo solus Episcopus verba consecrationis absolvit. Unde vitatur inconveniens supra obiectum: quia licet verba consecrationis prius ab aliquibus proferantur, tamen non operantur, nec effectum habent nisi in illo instanti, ad quod referuntur: et sic non fit consecratio super materiam praeconsecratam. Sed explicatio ista est voluntaria, et insufficiens: quoniam verba consecrationis sunt practica, et efficiunt, quod significant ad instar causae naturalis, quae ablato obice operatur: ergo non stat in potestate consecrantis impedire, quod verba statim operentur, vel quod operentur in alio tempore, ad quod, cum profert verba, refert intentionem: alias per verba de praesenti prolata posset consecrare in anno sequenti, quod est ridiculum, et absurdum.

Even if everyone agrees that more than one priest can consecrate the same host, they differ in how to explain this fact.

Some propose the theory that when they say the words, each priest should intend for them to take effect only at a later point.

Voluntaria: In this context, 'arbitrary.'

Recurrere vero pro isto speciali casu ad miraculosam aliquam, et extraordinariam providentiam Dei suspendentis effectum consecrationis nullum habet fundamentum; sed magis procedit contra communes institutionis sacramenti regulas, quas Theologus in suis discursibus sumere debet.

There is no evidence that warrants explaining a delayed effect of the words of consecration by a miraculous intervention of God.

Quod vero Marchinus, Pasqualigus, et quidam alii significaverunt non requiri concursum metaphysicum omnium consecrantium in eodem instanti: sed sufficere concursum moralem, sive quod inter unam, et alteram consecrationem non sit longa mora, ut virtute omnium consecrationum fiat transsubstantiatio: eodem motivo efficaciter refellitur. Quoniam verba consecrationis efficiunt, quod significant: ergo in illo reali, et metaphysico momento, in quo absolvuntur, operantur transsubstantiationem: atque ideo si tunc non efficiunt, nec efficient in alia duratione, ad quam ex intentione referantur: comparantur enim per modum causae naturalis, quae ubi non reperit obicem, necessario agit et ubi non est causa, non agit. Accedit specialis ratio in efficiendo sacramentum Eucharistiae, quae non procedit in aliis (quorum exemplo se declarant illi Auctores): nam in Baptismo v. g. requiritur applicatio materiae, et formae, ut fiat sacramentum operans suum effectum gratiae regenerantis: ad unionem autem materiae, et formae sufficit concursus moralis, sive quod inter eas non detur considerabilis mora:

A 'metaphysical' coming together means one at the exact same moment of time. A 'moral' coming together means at the same time (more or less) as far as common human judgment goes.

The Eucharist is distinct from other sacraments because the matter and form do not need to be applied to another subject.

sic enim adest moraliter totum signum causativum gratiae, in quo propria ratio talis sacramenti consistit. Sed in nostro casu non requiritur usus ad consecrationem materiae: sed ubi forma supra materiam aptam (ut supponitur), profertur, statim fit consecratio, sive conversio materiae in corpus, et sanguinem Christi. Idque magis confirmatur exemplo eius, qui solus consecrat: name ubi profert verba super panem, statim in ultimo prolationis momento fit transsubstantiatio, quin possit per ullam moram physicam, aut moralem ad aliud tempus differri: ergo idem continget, ubi plures consecrantes concurrunt: quod enim sint plures, est per accidens respectu cuiuslibet consecrantis. Unde nec patroni huius explicationis illam tueri valent, nisi recurrendo ad miraculum: quod tamen non esse admittendum iam diximus. Et Soto, qui hunc dicendi modum primus proposuerat in 4, distinctione 13, quaestione 1, artic. 2, § *Sed profecto*, illum tandem ut insufficientem ibidem deseruit.

Usus: In this case 'doing something' or 'doing anything' generically.

If a priest could delay the effect of the words of consecration with others present, he could do so alone. *Per accidens*: 'Accidental' in the sense of 'incidental.'

10. Quare idem proponit, et praefert aliam explicationem, nempe quod si ex omnibus in eo casu concurrentibus non omnes finiant consecrationis verba in eodem instanti; ille solus consecrat, sive sit Episcopus, sive alius, qui primus verba consecrationis absolvit. Curare tamen debent sacerdotes cum Episcopo celebrantes, ut si nequeant syllabati, et cum perfecta adaequatione cum Episcopo verba proferre; curent potius illa morosius, quam festinantius dicere,

ut si aliquis consecraturus sit, et est profecto aliquis, (cum omnes intendant absolute consecrare), sit potius ipse Episcopus, quam caeteri: quia illum maxime decet, cum debeat sacrificium perficere utramque speciem sumendo. Nemo autem peccat proferendo verba super hostiam praeconsecratam: quia omnes ignorant esse ab alio consecratam. Sed si quis adverteret alios iam absolvisse consecrationis verba, deberet ipse illa non continuare, sed cessare: quamvis practice loquendo tutum etiam sit illa absolvere cum intentione faciendi, quod tunc intendit Ecclesia. Unde vitantur inconvenientia, quae contra hanc consuetidinem supra obiiciebantur. Ita rem declarat Soto, cui subscribunt Vasquez disp. 118, cap. 4, Gaspar Hurtado, Lugo, Amicus, Sfortia, Diana, et Caspensis, apud Pradum quaest. 82, dub. 2, num. 15.

Nobis tamen hic dicendi modus non arridet: quia non tam vitat, aut excludit obiecta inconvenientia, quam devorat. Quod enim ille non reputat inconveniens nempe in tali casu contingere, quod Episcopus principaliter celebrans, non consecret, si scilicet alius sacerdos prius verba consecrationis absolvat; absurdissimum apparet: tum quia Episcopus est principaliter celebrans, et ali concelebrantes: tum quia ipse Episcopus perficit sacramentum sumendo species. *Deinde* iuxta praedictum dicendi modum contingens est, ut unus solus consecret panem, et alter solus

Non tam vitat … quam devorat: 'does not so much avoid … as swallows.' *Devorare* means 'to swallow' or 'to stomach' in the sense of 'to tolerate' or 'to accept.'

consecret vinum et alter denique, nempe Episcopus sumat utramque speciem: quae est inordinata confusio in eodem sacrificio, ut de se liquet. *Praeterea* malum ab intrinseco est proferre formam super indebitam materiam; ergo etiam est malum exponere se periculo proferendi formam super materiam indebitam: huic autem periculo manifeste se exponunt omnes simul celebrantes iuxta hanc explicationem; siquidem qui primus verba absolvit, ille consecrat, et caeteri supponunt materiam praeconsecratam: ergo peccant ita se gerendo. *Item* quando necessitas obligat ad proferendum formam super materiam dubiam, obligamur etiam ad habendum intentionem non absolutam, sed conditionatam: et aliter nos gerentes peccaremus peccato sacrilegii. Unde si quis haberet coram se plures formulas non consecratas cum certitudine morali, quod una earum, quam non cognoscit, esset consecrata, minime posset habere intentionem omnes, et singulas consecrandi; sed deberet procedere cum intentione excludente illam formulam, vel cum intentione conditionata consecrandi formulas, si consecratae non sunt, aut quae consecratae non sunt. Ergo pariter quando concurrunt plurimi sacerdotes ordinati ad consecrandum unam hostiam: cum multi eorum certi moraliter sint Episcopum, vel alium quem praeconsecrasse; nequeunt sine sacrilegio habere intentionem absolutam consecrandi. *Denique* quod maxime displicet in hoc dicendi modo, est manifesta

Formula: In this source, a small host for Holy Communion.

oppositio cum D. Thoma, et cum Innocentio Tertio, qui docent omnes tunc consecrantes debere suas intentiones referre ad idem instans consecrationis: quod praedicta sententia minime salvat: cum dicat omnes debere habere intentionem absolutam in consecrando, ita ut ille solus consecret, qui primus finiat verba consecrationis.

11. Relictis ergo his, et aliis dicendi modis, ille facilior, probabilior, et longe communior est, quem docent Victoria in *Summa, de Eucharistia*, numero 88, Petrus de Ledesma capite 9, conlusio 2, Nugnus, et Serra in praesenti articulo 2, Suarez disputatione 61, sectione 4, Coninckus, Filliucius, Villalobos, Castro Palao, et Dicastillo, quos refert, et sequitur Noster Franciscus capite 9, puncto 1, numero 5, Trullench, Granados, Tannerus, Martinus Praepositus, Aversa, Bernal, et alii communiter apud Pradum loco supra citato numero 13; statuit itaque ista sententia duo: primum omnes noviter ordinatos debere habere intentionem proferendi verba consecrationis iuxta voluntatem Ecclesiae; sive, et in idem recidit, proferendi illa verba meliori modo, et via, quibus fieri conveniat. Secundum huiusmodi sacerdotes debere habere intentionem consecrandi panem tunc praecise, quando simul cum Episcopo absolvant verba consecrationis in eodem momento; secus autem, si vel ante, vel post illum absolvant nam si hoc posterius contingat, solum intendunt talia verba proferre

The Authors' Own Explanation.

First Element.

Second Element.

instructionis, et caeremoniae gratia. Unde praedicta sacerdotum consecratio imbibit intentionem conditionatam ex parte obiecti conficiendi sacramenti, ubi simul cum consecratione Episcopi in eodem momento finitur; secus si non ita absolvatur. Et rationabiliter adhibetur haec conditio, ut in aliis rebus dubiis solet, ad evitandum scilicet proposita inconvenientia. Vitantur autem iuxta hunc dicendi modum omnia, quae opposuimus. Nam in primis salvatur, quod Episcopus, qui est principaliter celebrans, semper consecret: siquidem non aliter alii intendunt consecrare, quam si finiant simul cum Episcopo consecrationem: unde nulus praevenit effectum. Deinde nemo exponitur periculo proferendi verba consecrationis super materiam indebitam: quia nemo illam consecrare intendit, si absolvat post Episcopum, et inveniat materiam ab illo praeconsecratam. Dicere autem illa verba solius instructionis gratia, quod est dicere materialiter, et recitative, nullum est absurdum: praesertim ubi fit cum debita cautela, et reverentia ad observandum ritum Ecclesiae. Hoc itaque modo se debent habere sacerdotes noviter ordinati in consecratione panis. Et hoc etiam modo debent se proportionabiliter habere in consecratione calicis, nisi quod ulterius debent procedere sub alia conditione, nempe quod prius consecraverint panem; sive non consecrandi calicem, licet simul finiant cum Episcopo, si prius panem non consecraverint. Sic enim vitatur inconveniens, quod calix consecretur

Salvatur: *Salvare* often means 'to preserve' in the sense of being able to maintain an aspect or element of the explanation that one does not wish to leave out.

ab eo, qui non consecraverat panem. Quod si alicui videatur absurdum procedere sub tot conditionibus; advertat tum illas esse necessarias ad congruentius observandum hanc Ecclesiae consuetidinem: tum non esse necessarias explicite, ut quidam scrupulosus imaginari posset, sed sufficere pro implicito in illa una expressa intentione faciendi iuxta voluntatem Ecclesiae meliori modo, quo possit. Nec alia argumenta contra hunc dicendi modum occurrunt, quibus opus sit satisfacere: praesertim cum illud vulgatum de dependentia unius effectus a pluribus causis eiusdem ordinis, militet etiam in aliis explicationibus, et dicendi modis, et dilutum a nobis fuerit loco supra citato.

These conditions can be implicit.

CHAPTER XI
Sample Text II

In this text, Aquinas argues that the original sin committed by Adam and Eve was specifically one of pride.

ARTICULUS 1[64]

Utrum primum peccatum hominis fuerit superbia?

Objection 1.

Ad primum sic proceditur. Videtur quod superbia non fuit primum hominis peccatum. Discredere enim verba divina peccatum infidelitatis est. Sed peccatum hominis ex hoc processisse videtur quod verba Dei discredidit, vel de eis dubitavit, ut supra dictum est. Ergo primum peccatum hominis fuit infidelitas.

Objection 2. See especially Hebrews 11:10.

Praeterea, in spirituali aedificio primum fundamentum est fides, ut Hebr. 11 dicitur. Sed fidei opponitur infidelitas. Ergo etiam in progressu perditionis humanae primum peccatum fuit infidelitas, et non superbia.

Objection 3.

Praeterea, Rom. 5, 19, dicitur: *per inobedientiam unius hominis peccatores constituti sunt multi*, et loquitur ibi de peccato primo hominis; per peccatum enim mors in mundum intravit. Ergo primum peccatum est inobedientia.

Objection 4.

Praeterea, species peccati determinatur ex motivo ad peccandum. Sed mulier mota fuit ad peccandum ex delectabili secundum

---

64 Thomas Aquinas, *Super II Sent.*, d. 22, q. 1, a. 1.

gustum; unde dicitur Genes. 3, 6: *videns ergo mulier lignum* et cetera. Cum ergo circa delectabile ad esum sit gula, videtur quod primum hominis peccatum sit gula.

Esum: From *esus, -us* = 'eating.'

Praeterea, promissio Daemonis mulierem ad peccandum instigavit. Sed Daemon promisit perfectionem scientiae. Ergo ex appetitu scientiae peccavit. Sed immoderatus appetitus sciendi est curiositas. Ergo primum peccatum est curiositas.

Objection 5.

Praeterea, quicumque non facit illud quod facere tenetur, peccat peccato omissionis. Sed tenebatur homo in tentatione conferre de praecepto iniuncto: quia si contulisset, non peccasset. Ergo videtur quod peccato omissionis primo peccaverit.

Objection 6.

Tenebatur homo … conferre: 'Man was bound … to consider.'

Praeterea, primum peccatum hominis fuit radix et origo sequentium peccatorum. Sed, sicut dicitur 1 Timoth., ult., 10, *radix omnium malorum est cupiditas*. Ergo videtur quod primum peccatum fuit cupiditas, et non superbia vel elatio, ut in littera dicitur.

Objection 7.

Sed contra est quod dicitur Eccli. 10, 15: *initium omnis peccati superbia est*. Sed in primo peccato hominis omne peccatum initium sumpsit. Ergo primum peccatum fuit superbia.

On the Contrary 1.

Praeterea, Diabolus tentans hominem, sui imitatorem conatus est

On the Contrary 2.

reddere. Sed Daemon per superbiam peccavit, ut supra dictum est. Ergo et homo.

Respondeo dicendum, quod contingit quandoque in uno actu, plurium peccatorum deformitates inveniri: sed illa deformitas est principalior et formalior, complens speciem peccati, quae ex principali motivo relinquitur, in quod ordinantur alia: quia finis est id quod primum cadit in voluntate, ex qua est origo peccati; et ex fine actus morales specificantur; unde philosophus dicit in 5 *Ethic.* quod si aliquis moechatur ut accipiat lucrum, magis avarus, seu iniustus, quam moechus est. Secundum hoc dico, quod in primo peccato hominis multae deformitates apparent; unde Magister supra in eo notavit gulam, inanem gloriam, et avaritiam: propter quod unum peccatum multiplex potest dici; nihilominus tamen sunt omnia alia materialia respectu superbiae: quia ad finem excellentiae consequendae omnia ordinavit, sicut promissio Daemonis ostendit quae ad peccatum instigavit, dixit enim: *eritis sicut dii*, Genes. 3, 5. Et merito utriusque peccatum, et Daemonis et hominis a superbia incepit, quia omnium aliorum peccatorum defectus aliquis occasio solet esse: sola vero superbia est quae fundamentum ex perfectione sumit; unde Augustinus dicit, quod etiam bonis operibus insidiatur ut pereant.

Aquinas's Response. *Contingit quandoque ...*: 'It is sometimes the case ...'

Moral choices are classified into their different species on the basis of the goal.

Magister: Peter Lombard.

All the other sins (gluttony, vainglory, greed) are like the *material* principle of the first sin, whereas pride is like the *formal* principle. In other words, the gluttony, vainglory, and greed involved were all aspects of a choice that was fundamentally defined by pride.

See Augustine, Letter 221, *De Regula*.

Ad primum ergo dicendum, quod non crediderunt Deum falsum dixisse (hoc enim simpliciter infidelitatis fuisset), sed crediderunt forte alio modo intelligendum fore metaphorice, vel ad aliquid significandum esse dictum. Vel dicendum, quod ex ipsa elatione qua illud quod promittebatur appetebant, oculus mentis impeditus fuit ne actualiter veritatem divini dicti attenderent, secundum quod omnis malus aliquo modo ignorans est. Sed talis ignorantia vel dubietas, etiam credendorum, infidelitatem non facit.

Ad secundum dicendum, quod ordo compositionis est contrarius ordini resolutionis: quia quod est primum in compositione, est ultimum in resolutione: et ideo non sequitur quod si fides est prima in compositione aedificii spiritualis, infidelitas sit prima in resolutione eiusdem.

Ad tertium dicendum, quod inobedientia dupliciter sumitur: quandoque enim est speciale peccatum, quando scilicet ex contemptu praecepti aliquis specialiter peccat; quandoque autem sumitur prout est conditio generalis consequens omne peccatum mortale: cum enim praeceptum legis actus omnium virtutum ordinet, consequens est ut quodlibet vitium transgressionem annexam praecepti habeat, et inobedientiam: et sic dicitur: *per inobedientiam unius hominis peccatores constituti sunt multi.*

Reply to Objection 1.

Omnis malus ... ignorans: See Aristotle, *Nicomachean Ethics*, 3.1.1110b27–29.

Reply to Objection 2.

Ordo compositionis / resolutionis: On this inverse relationship in human choices, see Aristotle, *Nicomachean Ethics*, 3.3.1112b12–19.

Reply to Objection 3.

Romans 5:19.

Reply to Objection 4. Ad quartum dicendum, quod motivum gulae non fuit principale motivum, sed secundarium, et ordinatum ad aliud, ut dictum est.

Reply to Objection 5. Ad quintum dicendum, quod non peccavit mulier in hoc quod appeteret scientiam eorum quae ad ipsam non pertinebant, quia hoc curiositas fuisset; sed in hoc quod in scientia eminentiam desideravit, ut in hoc quodammodo Deo aequaretur.

Reply to Objection 6. Ad sextum dicendum, quod non tenebatur tunc conferre, quia etiam sine collatione poterat tentationi resistere. Vel dicendum melius, quod fuit ibi omissio, non prout est speciale peccatum, sed prout est consequens omne peccatum: in omni enim peccato commune est hoc quod aliquis non facit quod in se est ad resistendum peccato, quod si faceret, non peccaret.

Reply to Objection 7. Ad septimum dicendum, quod cupiditas tripliciter sumitur. Uno modo prout est speciale peccatum, et habet materiam specialem, scilicet bona ad usum vitae pertinentia, prout possidentur: et sic non est radix omnis peccati, nisi secundum quod infra Magister dicit, quod non est aliquod genus peccati quod non interdum ex avaritia oriatur. Secundo modo dicitur cupiditas, ut est generale peccatum, prout est immoderatus appetitus habendi quodcumque, vel scientiam, vel

CHAPTER XI

possessionem, vel quodlibet aliud: et hoc modo supra Magister dixit in primo peccato hominis esse avaritiam: et hos duos modos ponit Augustinus 11 *super Genes*. Tertio modo, prout non est peccatum, sed radix peccati, prout dicit quamdam pronitatem appetitus ut inclinetur ad aliquid inordinate appetendum in actu. Et constat quod primo modo, ut cupiditas est speciale peccatum, homo ex avaritia non peccavit.

CHAPTER XII
Sample Text III

In this excerpt, Jean-Baptiste Gonet (1615–81) introduces a discussion about the *lumen gloriae* ('light of glory'), which is a modification given to the human mind in heaven so that it can see God's essence directly. The discussion boils down to the question of what kind of contribution the human mind makes to its intellectual vision of God. Is it totally passive? If not, what is it doing exactly?

ARTICULUS V.[65]

Quomodo concurrat intellectus lumine gloriae elevatus ad visionem beatificam, an ut causa principalis, vel instrumentalis?

§. I.
Praemittitur quod apud omnes est certum.

XLV. Suppono tamquam certum, et ab omnibus fere Theologis contra Nominales receptum: Deum non producere visionem beatificam in intellectu Beati, ipso mere passive se habente, sed intellectum creatum lumine gloriae elevatum, active in eam influere.

Nominales: 'Nominalists.'

As in classical Latin, the expression *se habere* is common, and can usually be translated by 'to be.'

Influere: 'To have an influence on,' but in this context, it could be translated more fluidly as 'to contribute to.'

Ratio fundamentalis est, quia visio beata est actio vitalis: ergo debet active procedere ab intellectu creato, lumine gloriae perfuso. Consequentia patet: in hoc enim differt natura vivens ab inanimata, quod illa se movet ab intrinseco, et est principium active influens in suas operationes: altera vero solum ab extrinseco movetur, et in se recipit motum ab alio productum. Antecedens vero probatur primo, quia in Scriptura, Beati videntes Deum dicuntur vivere vita aeterna; iuxta illud Ioan. 17. *Haec*

Proof of the Logical Entailment.

Consequentia: The logical 'entailment' or 'consequence.' *Illa*: When comparing two things, 'the former.'

First Proof of the Antecedent.

---

65   From Jean-Baptiste Gonet, *Clypeus theologiae Thomisticae* I, tract. 2, disp. 3, a. 5.

est vita aeterna, ut cognoscant te Deum verum. Secundo, quia videre Deum, est intelligere, et cognoscere illum ut in se est: sed intellectio et cognitio, actio vitalis est, ut constat; sicut esse intellectivum et cognoscitivum, dicit gradum vitae perfectissimum; ergo visio beatifica, actio vitalis est.

Second Proof of the Antecedent.

Esse here should be taken as a substantive: 'being.'

Tertio, sicut gratia habitualis est participatio vitalitatis divinae per modum radicis, ita etiam lumen gloriae est formalis participatio vitae divinae per modum principii proximi: unde sicut homo iustus, per gratiam et charitatem vivit vita supernaturali, ita et Beatus, videndo Deum vivit vita aeterna et beata.

Third Proof of the Antecedent.

Per modum + genitive of X: This can usually be translated 'as X.' In this case, 'as proximate principle.'

XLVI. Confirmatur primo ex Tridentino sess. 6. can. 4. definiente, liberum arbitrium non se habere mere passive in ordine ad actus quibus ad iustificationem disponitur: sed non alia ratione, ad actus praedictos non comparatur mere passive liberum arbitrium creatum, nisi quia sunt vitales, et consequenter debent procedere ab intrinseco: ergo cum visio beatifica vitalis sit, debet etiam a principio intrinseco active concurrente procedere.

First Supporting Proof.

XLVII. Confirmatur secundo: Si Beati nihil agerent in visione beatifica, frustra daretur eis lumen gloriae, frustra essentia divina eorum mentibus uniretur per modum speciei impressae et expressae: ad quid enim illa visionis beata principia,

Second Supporting Proof.

Per modum speciei impressae et expressae: Basically, in the beatific vision, God's essence itself takes the

CHAPTER XII

si nullam eliciant intellectionem, sed mere passive se habeant? Et si Deus tantum in illis, et non per illos operatur, ad quid elevatur eorum intellectus? Hoc praesupposito tamquam certo, inquirunt Theologi modum quo intellectus lumine gloriae elevatus, active influit in visionem beatam; an ut causa principalis, vel instrumentalis?

place of human concepts and ideas, so that God is seen in the mind directly.

Segue to a more precise question.

CHAPTER XIII
Resource List

Note: Some of the older works can be found on Google Books.

Deferrari, Roy J. *A Lexicon of Saint Thomas Aquinas.* Loreto Publications, 2004.

Glazier, Michael. *Consecrated Phrases: A Latin Theological Dictionary.* 3rd ed. Collegeville, MN: Liturgical Press, 2013.

Goclenius, Rudolph. *Lexicon philosophicum, quo tanquam clave philosophiae fores aperiuntur.* Frankfurt: Typis viduae Matthiae Beckeri, impensis Petri Musculi et Ruperti Pistorii, 1613.

Gredt, Josef. *Elementa philosophiae Aristotelico-Thomisticae.* Editio 13 recognita et aucta ab Euchario Zenzen. 2 vols. New York: Herder, 1961.

Mantello, F. A. C., and A. G. Rigg, eds. *Medieval Latin: An Introduction and Bibliographical Guide.* Washington, DC: CUA Press, 1996.

Micraelius, Johann. *Lexicon philosophicum terminorum philosophis usitatorum.* Stettin: Impensis Jeremiae Mamphrasii, Bibliop., Typis Michaelis Höpfneri, 1661.

Muller, Richard A. *Dictionary of Latin and Greek Theological Terms: Drawn Principally from Protestant Scholastic Theology.* 2nd ed. Grand Rapids, MI: Baker Academic Group, 2017.

Nunn, H. P. V. *An Introduction to Ecclesiastical Latin.* Cambridge: University Press, 1922.

Signorellus, Nuntius. *Lexicon peripateticum philosophico-theologicum in quo scholasticorum distinctiones et effata praecipua explicantur.* Pignatelli, 1872.

Wuellner, Bernard. *A Dictionary of Scholastic Philosophy.* 2nd ed. Milwaukee: Bruce, 1966.

———. *Summary of Scholastic Principles.* Chicago: Loyola, 1956.

Made in the USA
Monee, IL
25 August 2020